Ghost in the Archive

Ghost in the Archive

Jennifer
LOYD

Printed in the United States of America

ISBN: 979-8-9883272-4-0

Published by Conduit Books & Ephemera
788 Osceola Avenue
Saint Paul, Minnesota 55105
www.conduit.org

Book design by Scott Bruno/b graphic design

Distributed by Itasca Books
www.itascabooks.com

Cover images: Didier Descouens, *Egg of Pallas's Rosefinch*, collection of Perrin de Brichambaut, Muséum de Toulouse; Naumann, *Naturgeschichte der Vögel Mitteleuropas*. Courtesy Wikimedia Foundation.

CONTENTS

III. MARINE ORIGINS

IV. THE DOMAIN OF PERFECT AFFECTION

V. WE'RE STILL LYING

The sea is no less beautiful to our eyes just because
we know sometimes boats sink.

—Simone Weil

There is no single story.

—Chimamanda Ngozi Adichie

Remember all those loves your fantasies
created for you.

—C. P. Cavafy

I Want to Tell Rachel Carson about Centralia, Pennsylvania, & 24-Hour Gas Stations

Take desire, for example.
I am always searching
for the hidden entrance
in the trunk of the riven tree.
One minute, mistletoe is a parasite,
the next, a collaborator.
I imagine the entanglement of all
energy on its way to outer space
must sound, to the universe,
like the music playing in line
for Space Mountain.
All the things I've thrown away
in gas station bathrooms—
like the thrice-wrapped pregnancy test
taken at 4 a.m.—
I imagine they must share space in the atmosphere
with the ash of the letters she burned.

I

NOW, AGAIN

Remember, Body

two women in the night water
write on each other
phosphorescent words.

Conflation

An escaped fundamentalist,
I just let myself out
of the gate one day.

Left the community table,
the forks in their due place,
the long-enough hemlines.

Shame, that smoke-smell,
clung to my hair
(as did a husband).

To learn what to do
with my many limbs,
I watched celebrities.

I was attracted to women
with a tourniquet smile
(think Agent Scully,

think Martha Stewart,
think Athena—sprung fully armored
from Zeus's head).

I enrolled in community college,
where I read *Silent Spring*, and recognized
something it would take years to see:

a woman in her authority,
in rage and loneliness.
A woman in love with women.

And though I never wondered
about Aldo Leopold's
home life, I wondered if Carson

had been happy,
or if she too had watched
from the doorways.

I asked the archives,
the biographies,
the tidepools.

They were silent.
And teeming with life.

I worried about conflation,
but I wanted—
still want—confluence.

Pygmalion

O, marble Rachel, how shall I dress you,
        in your own drab browns or this stolen green pantsuit?

What will I play you: rain on a sea urchin's drum
        or Tchaikovsky's Sixth—the open-heart surgery of it?

Will I bend you over the microscope's sterile light?
        Will I *chassé* you from closet to pedestal and back again?

Chisel in fist, I imagine want
        onto you and then identify with it.

I am a body tearing into a body.
        I am equipping you, after the fact, with a sway bar

for what's coming—vine-black nights,
        charred grapevines and salt, me at your feet.

Jenn Loyd Discovers That Nothing Bad Ever Happened at Rachel Carson's Childhood Home

In fact, the only things to see are the sassafras
tree with its thumb-sized bees, the seasonal
red-breasted robin invasion. Some notable doorglass.

So I, who pathologize everything, am out
of place, even though I managed to visit
in the hour between rain
and more rain.

I came to see the underbelly
of the heart-shaped rock
(certified maggot-free),
the trap door leading to the bottomless well
of motherly love, and the father-archetype
misting between branches in the orchard.

I came prepared for the mess and swash
of biography. The docent likes questions,
but she doesn't ask them. She strikes a tone
when the word "homosexual" comes up—
two parts *no,* one part
why does this keep coming up?

The river, down where the stacks smoke,
would be just visible from the house in winter.
"In the recession," she says,
"townsfolk voted to close this place."
Meanwhile, on the edge of the mown lawn,
a vine bends back to climb itself.

Fundament

As a girl, I lived on the edge
of various violences.

Chased to thresholds, pushed
into storage rooms, measured
by the width of a strap, or watched
like a clay pigeon.

"No man should have to be so
tempted," they told me.

I Want to Ask the Archive about Rape Culture

Archive, what if my wish is to stand in the driveway
& not be ogled.
By the trees, by the Chevy, by
the mailman's dog.
Archive, what if I own a scarf
knitted by a man convicted of rape.
Green and beige.
And what if
I wear it around my neck.
When is he
a rapist—
while raping or forever.
Archive, if I live in a rape culture,
what do you
live in.
I worry
there were periods of time
when people were having rape,
but calling it sex.
Or not calling it anything.
Archive, what to do
with the word "monster."
Wait, where are my question
marks.
The driveway.
The scarf.
The world.
Aren't these
questions.

Cult(ure)

Words we did not use: “cult,”
“evangelical,” “Protestant.”
Our lexicon bent instead
between service and conversion:
“territory,” “ministry,” “the truth.”
We walked house-to-house,
knocking on doors,
under that Florida sky—
a bluewhite lid
that trapped the carnal heat
against my skin.
Our long sleeves and stockings
were meant to impress
others into self-conscription.
I never saw the ruler that measured
the length of my skirt,
just the hatch marks
of my various infractions.
The point of marching
is to lose the self,
to warp the loose
thread back into the weft.

Against Historical Depictions of Two Unmarried People of the Same Gender Who Lived Together for Years

Bitter milk
on my lips.
Oh, the intelligence
of the body.
One voice is a marrow bridge.
Strung together,
they spandrel,
hard as unheard testimony.

Part-Time Stalker

I had my second and last panic attack
on Route 27 in Maine. I had driven
across the continent to that tree-heavy highway
to poke at photographs you took, to triangulate
the location of your winter house
from clues in your letters about a bend
in the Sheepscot River. I walked the coastal
path a half mile from your home,
wishing you would startle me
by appearing—apparition.
Wishing you might lick me like a mother
cat, that you might like me,
part-time stalker of your archives.
Wishing that, like me,
you would have found comfort in the fact
of that water wetting the feet of a woman
fifty years later. Your house—place where you
made salad and masturbated and took that photo
of the wave in its seven textures—
was shuttered. Milkweed pods
in the front yard were the gray of a ghost town,
but an hour after sunset, black shapes
surfaced and rolled in the dolphinless river.

II

SILENT SPRING

Remember, Body

First, single syllables:
once, you, breath,

then one of them tries *lavender*
and runs out of collarbone.

Eight Elegies for Omission

1) Mown grass, a tulip bouquet: spring is sliced veins of phloem. 2) Heavy clouds clique together in occasional grays. 3) Across the road children play the exquisite-scream game. 4) An elm is urgent and half white with rice-paper seeds. 5) *These dandelions are record-breaking,* a girl says. 6) The neighbor kid plays with his hockey *stick-stick-stick-stick* (like the second hand on a clock) from 4 p.m. until the blueblack hour. 7) The pain of abundance. 8) Willow tree—depressed cousin of bamboo—limpid till wind.

And you, Dear History?
Dear limpid, rice-paper History,
what else is missing?

Epistles in Which Rachel Carson Uses Romantic Language That Will Worry Biographers Claiming Her Relationship with Dorothy Freeman Was Strictly Platonic: A Cento

My Darling,   to step off the train into your arms   "ifs"   "whys"   loves[1]

If we could have   even a little time   Christmas[2]   linger[3]

No more till   when?[4]   awful if it was only one   you say not to   I imagine[5]

Leaping   the mail truck   breath   we have to   summer   need[6]

You, the white hyacinth   I invest[7]   we would have[8]

Rattle my heart   not long[9]   hours / hours[10]

My path   you[11]   tell me   it is   I am   we are   heart.[12]

---

[1] December 11, 1953
[2] December 21, 1953
[3] December 26, 1953
[4] January 21, 1954
[5] January 25, 1954
[6] January 30, 1954
[7] February 6, 1954
[8] February 17, 1954
[9] March 9, 1954
[10] June 27, 1954
[11] November 8, 1954
[12] December 25, 1954

Two Women Agree to Burn Certain Letters Designated "Strong Box"

As pieces of the world
we are a problem for,
is it any wonder—

this impulse to destroy
these parts
of ourselves?

Slap

A slap across the face is one way

of saying how dare you.

A dare. A slap. A mother. A daughter.

The skill for self-pruning is

inherited.

What a mother does

is as important as what she says.

My mother hid words.

She strongboxed them.

Ashed them.

I ate the ashes.

The words lined the lining of my intestines.

Little ulcer seeds.

Phobophobia

with language from Christopher Okigbo and Carolyn Gerald

fear of plums, wild, in your backyard; or

fear of the bite, of needless repentance; of renovating the universe; or

fear of your neighbor, the heft of her breasts as she walks, or

fear of clocks with weighted arms; or

fear of that stranger, your mother, asking about the purple ghost stain
on your lips; or

fear of realizing there have always been plums, wild in your backyard,
along with the whirring birds, the vine-on-vine sidelines,
the night-steps where your feet found
what your hands couldn't;

but, most of all, fear of the sea sinking the ship, its gold crop ungathered

Fundamentalism

a cult can be identified
by two little girls
in a Kroger
wearing a certain kind
of ordinary dress

a cult can be found by a mother
looking for what to tell her toddler
about god

a cult can be
created through a deeply, deeply
shared story

a cult can be avoided (how quickly I spot them walking:
a sidewalk, a Starbucks, a campus plaza—
it's the hem length, the bookbags,
the aroma of agenda)

I still love people,
people who practice explaining
that they are not in a cult

amazing—even
the tiniest thread in me
was enough
to leave
(thank you, tiny thread)

I left
I did
I managed
this thing I now identify
as *out*

Strongbox Letter #46

One day I hope to find you
between these words— *island, barrier, pearls on clavicle.*

One day you'll tell me how
you stayed on that beach
till tide's retreat to count wild horses.
How the money's in mammals,
but you only wanted to catch the sea's
brine between your boots—
coquina pulp and crabs the size of the eye's iris.
One day I won't blame you
for lying, for cutting yourself out
of the photograph.

One day I'll find that beach.
The sky and sea will twin
at the horizon.
I won't be surprised by the wilderness
of it all. I will sit on the sand
until I can't tell hand from frond.
Ships will come in, their lights pulsing
nothing like moon-glow.

Islomania

Rachel Carson and I went to Lesbos once forever.
On that island with its strange mangrove rind,

populated entirely by the ghosts
of historical women, I asked her

about being raised to take
up as little space as possible.

About a single baked sweet potato for dinner—
no butter and only the tongue's memory of sugar.

We were unmapped and true there, apt to change
lagoons abruptly. Carson swam

the sentient shoreline, soaked through
with thoughts of boundaries,

of bayan arms cradling a floody plain,
of runes and paper rivers. A crush

is the windy edge of life.
What an embarrassment to want

people, to want abstractions and their opposites,
to confess I stood in the narrow stairs of her childhood

home and tried to push my longing for her
down the bare wood treads.

The problem with history is how to collect flotsam
from what never happened but did.

Why Rachel Carson Was Not a Painter

Because she had no eye for the little house of light diffused inside
an orange peel.

Because she escaped Pittsburgh, a glue factory, fricative rivers of carp.

Because her relentless quest was not west, but the low, low-tide land.

Because she wrote poems first (quiet, clotted, petal-fall).

And because most surfaces, really any skin, would do.

Also elegy, elegies.

And hypotheses: armistice, the pine woods, those horses' inorganic
arc to glue.

How she twisted under the soundthumb of "rind" and "Dardanelles."

A porous boundary for the war body is what she wanted.

To pour saltwater over her feet, and, oh, god—industry, love, the fact
of ocean.

III

MARINE ORIGINS

Remember, Body

That time of year, dawn arrives earlier
every day. It arrives and arrives and arrives.

Historical Gaydar

A game I play.

Was she,
was RC,
queer?

Queer, before it was safe to be?

Which is to say,
some incalculable date in the future?

A Crush Is a Scream

Rachel Carson and her mother, Maria, stand in the foyer like two columns of steam.

The DSM has labelled homosexuality a mental illness.

The mother doesn't like women; the daughter is a furious bird.

Thank god for dreams: how many more nights like last night will Rachel get?

In her dream, the other woman's jaw is a razor denuding a path down Rachel's back.

An embarrassment of clean.

The opposite of vertigo.

If tension is a body's currency,

a collar is meant to be undone.

A scream, meant to be heard.

Mother Energy

It starts with a mother in a clapboard kitchen—
        she battens down
the bread rag and sifts remnants

each night in the oildim light. Her unborn child,
        a girl, trails on the umbilical
vein, exacting and curious already.

When she muscles her future-famous daughter into being,
        it happens—no, not just form,
that glorious, temporary miracle,

but the energy between life and form, what makes
        this child meteoric,
as across the continent, electricity is blooming.

Neutrinos pass right through the downy black hair
        and the afterbirth.
It's dark matter that yokes the universe. All of it. Together.

Rachel Carson Considers the Family Homestead

Winter, that great destroyer of a schoolgirl's
schedule. Outside, her father & brother break

ice, bank snow to insulate the barn. A fox cartwheels
onto its prey & leaves grow into mold.

School is closed & in the kitchen gloam,
she peels beets. Knobby globes,

red & warm, their brine glad to bleed
across her knuckles. She worries each root

into a fawn's heart & does strange, slippery
medicine on their epicardia. The truth is

if a girl doesn't return to school

(Oh, slide-rules, Oh, high marks, Oh,
ticker-tape of recitations)

if a girl doesn't return to school

no one will ask. Another truth—she hates peeling beets.
No skin ever said, "I'll just slip right off."

Fundamental

Over breakfast, her mother reads to her
books with Sunday words.

Soldier is a popular metaphor,
and she is in training.

A blockade, by definition, stops the flow of bread
on the same earth that grows vines
thicker than a soldier's arm.

She writes poems with pilots,
not questions. Parents encourage asking
but only about certain things.

People are being killed over words,
and she doesn't know how
to take them any less seriously.

In the woods, she wonder-broods—
fern's articulated blade, sweet gum's inquisition,
verbena's umbrella.
Vines query a trunk's tender architecture with largess.

It's lonely, but the only work.

Latent

The girl reads the thesaurus—
sanctuary has *temple* and *shrine,* even *asylum—*
but *laboratory* has no synonym.
Maybe *the woods,* she thinks.
Or, unless one accounts for verbs.
In the deer's nest, then, she *lays*
down. The word for this place, she *remembers.*
She *counts*
pine varieties, *identifies*
natives and invasives, *notes*
oak leaves *straining*
light into shade, *observes*
how walnuts—common as quarter moons—*wump*
the mud in their climp-clomp way.

Genealogy

Everything rations. But her great-great-
grandmother's laugh was a watercourse: rough, carousing
with the shore, stopping short of flood.

A great-aunt dug into the Alleghenies,
springs in the hillside. Grim magic.

Her great-grandmother, with magnolia
hands, healed wild, indignant cardinals.

One grandmother disowned the sea,
warned of danger in the cold shine. Buzz-cut her hair
with her dead husband's razor.

Someday she will want what they once wanted—
to be naked in a field with azaleas.

It's not too much.

Some Mothers Are as Lighthouse to Ship

All warning. No shelter.

Rachel Carson's mother: three children, an ill husband,
clapboard walls, inherent intelligence, no degree, no running water.

She sold the family china for Rachel's tuition, gave her
a ledger book with inked-in prices and instructions
to subtract every pencil and lemon ice.

If you get pregnant, you'll be worth nothing.

Since the first daughter, whose name god forgot
to record in the bible, this has been going on—

this mother-want

for their daughters. This selling
of china and its cabinets,

this pricing of red as pink.

If I catch you
under the stairs
with that girl again,
I'll kill you.

Leaving Pennsylvania for the Sea

Most nights the moon
isn't full. Rain in degrees
of hard and rage.
Field edges where the beans
failed. Houses in various states
of disrepair and love—
a wood pile slid sideways,
a path worn to a rope swing,
hydrangea heads
left to nod at winter.
The pastor insisted
we were created
in Sunday's image.
And sometimes the sun
does shine for an hour
before smog sews
shut the sky.
On the coldest days
a frozen dust lifts behind the trucks
bound for the glue factory.
It whitens their cargo
of old horses.

Empiricism

this marine biologist was afraid of boats

        she believed in the necessity   of water

while wishing for shore   wanted to love

        water   without being   on it or in it

she tossed overboard   messy feelings

        the girl at school   the homestead for sale

she sent a sounding line to an underwater prairie

        sampled the poorly-sampled wilderness there

floated over a ghosted coastal shelf   (grave sailors

        masked as mermen)

the sea writes humans out of its narrative

        like October sheds light

water chewed up by keel

        that bleach-smell   on it or in it

Sinking or Swimming Can Help an Organism

two ways to dive—
like a whale or not

the "bends" can twist
the spine like sponge

but "dive," said William Beebe
(he of bathysphere fame)
and Rachel Carson agreed

how else would she see
the sea the strong sea

and the tiny particulars
gills tentacles lamellae

make their grand theory of ocean

she weighed 120 pounds
the helmet weighed 84
rain or sea-spray freckled the visor
she descended ladder-deep and remained boat-tethered

that being enough

the water's green throttle ::: wet tender chemistry :::
seaweed tinseling her fingers ::: alive as information ::: hard as
any eclipse

blood's ordinary oxygen
stereo stereo of breath

Pantoum for 1939

"Decline," the *New York Times* reported,
"W. B. Yeats remains in bed."
His heart condition.
The prophet's question: how hard did I knock?

W. B. Yeats remained in bed,
And Europe would be exhumed and buried again.
The prophet's question: how hard should I knock?
Delay is virtual manslaughter.

A twice-buried continent,
Where bullet was touch and metamorphosis.
Delay was manslaughter.
Which do those in power prefer—

The bullet, the touch, or the metamorphosis?
Sanctions provoked a climate of war.
Which will the future prefer,
The convenient lie of the white page or the prophecy?

That was a time when climate sanctions might have been enough.
There were ice floes near County Sligo—
Then came white lies, white pages, convenient prophecies.
Rachel Carson wrote of fewer salmon, the last heath hen.

The ice flowed away from Sligo.
The female gaze is one of surveillance,
And Carson wrote of earth's watery glance.
Bank up your memory, she said: the river, the mayfly, the redhead duck.

Her female gaze surveilled.
What she saw: people were choosing rapture over nature.
Remember the riverbank, the mayfly, the redhead duck
Slaughtered by every day's delay.

"Choose nature over the rapture,"
Urged Carson's heart's condition.
Everyday slaughter.
The *New York Times* reports decline.

Rachel Carson Speaks on "The Rachel Carson Problem"

They label me lady: lady-writer, lady-wader,
lady-lab rat. There is no more milk

in my breasts than in a Parker House roll, so they write *quiet,*
spinster, problem. They note

my pink lipstick. What they mean is that there are
pinkwomen and redwomen, that red

should be paled into pink, that I should be
more like my lipstick. (There is no single

English word for pale blue.) In grade school,
I wrote RL Carson on each draft.

Now a fan letter addresses me as "Sir,"
my correspondent unwilling to discuss biology

with a woman. Later—my name on the meeting agendas
of multinational petrochemical companies:

"How to Answer Rachel Carson"
and "The Rachel Carson Problem."

The sin of *Silent Spring*—
that I didn't prefer a neutral tone.

IV

THE DOMAIN OF PERFECT AFFECTION

Remember, Body

One of those women shivers
like a fortune teller
married to a doctor
on the eve of an epidemic.

The Domain of Perfect Affection

1955. New York City. Rachel Carson and Dorothy Freeman share two nights at the Barbizon-Plaza Hotel[1]

I.

A room overlooking Central Park,
stainless as an autoclave.
Implied intimacy in its twoness:
beds, drapes, chairs.

Rachel can be comfortable here.
She has chased *smart* and *sterile*
since she first learned the words.
Sterile allows for smart—no time spent swabbing mud,
no toes twisted on debris. Leave the dirt in childhood.

---

1 *1855. Fontainebleau. Rosa Bonheur and Nathalie Micas name their château the "Domain of Perfect Affection."*

II.

Dorothy chose this hotel
for the Art Deco spires gilding
the roof. Rachel believes
in entropy, not alchemy,
how once you have something
you begin to lose it. They argue
over the unmade bed, about what it means

to want the intimacy but not the mess.[1]

---

[1] At night in the studio, Rosa paints
beneath chandeliers
that drip from vaulted ceilings.
Taxidermy clots the walls:
bears, gazelles, ocelots,
an ibis perches on driftwood.
Outside the wolf moon
shines on the juniper
that curtains the caged lion.
Silently, the big cat curls backwards
into such sleep.

III.

Rachel is in New York to explain the sea to an audience of hundreds.[1]

Rachel is shy.

To reduce the amount of speaking in her speech,

she plays an extended recording of shrimp speaking to other shrimp:

a series of squeaks and snaps as they push and pull their claw joints out of socket—

an underwater articulation.

Dorothy is in New York to explain Rachel to herself.

---

[1] Bonheur's "The Horse Fair" is a painting of animal force
and human economy. A meeting of equal rages
(Percherons vs. reins).

The thinnest bridle laid across
seventeen hands of agile muscle and wild
intelligence eventually restrains.

IV.

New York intimidates me,
Dorothy thinks, and not why you'd expect:

not the traffic, not the air's angry particulates.
No, it's the proximity to art,

to exhibition and frames, the hidden nail in the wall.

But a hotel room is a condensery.
Room service ("dining in your bedroom")

and the day's accoutrements:
pen, empty glass, extra pillow.

Except Rachel left, and the sunrise didn't last.[1]

---

[1] A bridle is palimpsest (that favorite tool
of the painter raised in poverty)
laid across a neck bent mid-plunge,
one white blaze on a furrowed head,
the sinews' articulation alive.

V.

My dear—how funny we are—with our little joke—an assignation—friends—a joke—our long-awaited rendezvous—your book tour, my daily duties for the Daughters of Southport Summit—and somehow our roles requiring the same city the same day—assignation!—you taught me that word—a joke—a falling together—of friends—the desk clerk knew more than we—hooded his eyes—placed key on counter—*"don't you have any luggage"*—us laughing—no one I know knows that type of girl—in the elevator—assignation—ha—in the room—only bed and desk—and a painting of violets—legs of our stockings tangled over the shower curtain, four shoes by the door—*how many books did you sign today*—single glass of sherry on the bed—shared—even then—never drunk—you—bluehour—not even then—we undress—two robes—I never—wear underwear to bed—I know—pre-touch—then—and—and—oh—[1]

---

[1] The torqued length of a leg,
fur shading hooves,

tails pinned against their rumps
like hair hastily put up after love.

VI.

faint tang of iodine
re-wet mascara
smudges her stomach
curls undone
by her hands
so late, the lace
salt brines their one mouth
no-hum of the heater they didn't need

the full moon skirts
the windowsills
they close their eyes
at such discretion[1]

---

1 oh let's blue our bodies under the juniper again let's be moonsound silver rising bottles full to burst let's pull the tide over us where we lay the smell black and alive and let's spend salt to get more salt

VII.

taste is the opposite

of erasure

though blurred edges

blur further

the skin

organ smears into its full

inhabitance of skin[1]

---

[1] While in the orchard,
the trees' roots work private songs
from the creek.
The gasp of a quince
dropping to the grass.

VIII.

Afterward, letters:

Dorothy's effusiveness,

Rachel's reticence.

Stillborn nights,

blinds down

as though weighted

by coins.[1]

---

[1] No. Begin again, with a sudden bed, the white page of it. Appropriate, the September fireworks—surprise noise and light borrowed from July. *Are you okay with this?* she asked, the first time her hand in the dark found hers. A shadow calendar. Days were an energy-saving dance, and only nights counted. To constellate is to make meaning, no matter how momentary. *Be more,* they told the gunpowder, *be more,* they ordered the stars. And they were.

V

WE'RE STILL LYING

Remember, Body

The tide always rolls back out,
and with its wash,
any creature without
something to hold onto.

False Negative

Oh, and the private amphitheater
of her ear. Fear of loss turned turned her mouth

hard. But there was a bumper-car joy
in kissing her, while on the jetty, a passing bike

lifted a wake of leaves. She was afraid

of taproots, their fixed pride.
Daily, the projection of *normal.*

First her torso, then her life, she feared,

would articulate
into a wall. The unsaid.

The Plural of Anecdote Is Data

What thoughts I have of you tonight, Rachel Carson. Though that could be said of most nights. Tonight, though, tonight a man is dying. He has cast his last ballot (late-blooming liberal), while I make store-trips, wipe countertops, read. He's dying, as he lived, like a man in the woods with a bear on his scent—hands up through the brush. He rejects the Gatorade, the memories of his earlier votes, the latent fear and hate of his childhood.

When he was twelve years old, his parents sent him for electric shock therapy. There was concern he was gay. This according to neighbors; the family's still not talking. But you, Rachel, you who went on only one date (the senior prom) with a boy, your limbs and heart lay dormant until thirty years later, until Dorothy, your neighbor, the woman whose arms you wanted to step off the train into, the woman who left her own parties to pine outside for you. What did you know, Rachel, and when did you know it?

Everyone cross-examines from deep within their own trench, but I can't sift fact from myth. I can't determine if Queen Victoria labeled lesbians mythical, and therefore exempt from the anti-homosexual laws of 1885, or was the myth that she ever declared *anything* about lesbians?

I realize that was before your time, Rachel, but I worry women self-edit. Did you?

Sometimes, for the private nest it opens in my chest, I lie. Is that the same?

Rachel, what verb to label my love for this man, now that he's dying? It's not love that worries me, but the way we grammar feeling, grope for the perfect tense.

When you were fifty years old, you had loved Dorothy for four years, but in a few more, you'd lose your life because of a lie, a doctor's false diagnosis of benign. If words aren't enough, how much are we reduced? Asking questions remains a radical act.

Unlike this dying man, I've never wanted to die. Though once, flying cross-country and in the midst of an extramarital affair—untethered to earth except for desire's gravity—I considered that it might be easier if the plane crashed. Then I wouldn't have to do the work of delineating my wanting and articulating it. But that was self-pity, rather than a wish to be edited out of the plane's detritus.

My dying friend has never been himself, and so his relationship to his own life has always been tenuous. What if he had died the first time he wanted to? The second? In this last week of life, cancer paws at his lungs' gravel. He accepts the clean knife, the right cuts. I am a tourist in his life, as I am in yours, Rachel. As I am, too often, in my own. I pick through these degrees of debris, while he fixes his gaze on a point so distant I know everything I see is palimpsest.

How to Love a Famous Woman

She's eating fruit over the sink again,
so the summer houses must be empty.

Yesterday, the last veeries, her favorite birds.
"Always make a note of where," she said.

(The fallow road between their houses.)
One sounds out: *veer-veer-veer,*

"Or was it jeer?"
Birds, chaff, her—spiraling south.

State line like a hemisphere.
She was foraging, forgetting

the wings which could return her.
Could she even handle her year-round?

"Listen," she said. "Coppery echo, tin soliloquy."
Some somatic sweetness brushes past her

on its way down the hill
as she remembers her hands on her.

She looks, brush-shuffles. No
freckled chests, no cinnamon wings,

only the last of the wood-wasps.
"Trace your hand on a piece of paper,"

she said, "and I'll buy you a ruby ring."
The path back—littered with fallen plums.

Deathbed

Professor—the ruby pleasure
of calling her that
when you no longer
had to. She who
showed you moths
the size of your pinkie nail.
How to diagram
the jaguars, raccoons,
great northern bears
that populated her course.
To listen
for the girl leaving
the laundry each midnight
singing, her voice
a shade lighter than the hour—
sonic inoculation
against hesitation.
Who let you confess
the vowels of "butterfly"
in Russian, Spanish, Norwegian.
She who pushed aside the papers
on her desk and who said *Oh, oh*
when she caught a fish.
The bottles by her bed—
like a Galilean thermometer
of drugs, the old miracle
of suspension.
(At any point, the state of medicine
is less advanced
than it will be
in a year.) Also
by her bed,
your last letter, with its
Stay, its *Love*.

Cento in Which the Word "Cloud" Is Replaced by the Word "Crush"

from and for Rachel Carson

the birth of the Crush is relatively peaceful and simple
water molecules blossom into the fabric of Crush

the Crush puffs up to extraordinary heights
the Crush towers off of radar screens ... a 70,000-foot giant ...
twice Everest

what of the Crush itself

it is the high-riding Crush that first beholds the sunrise

fog is nothing but a Crush so near, it touches

the science of a Crush shows how warning signals are hung
in the sky for all to read

the flier who can read the Crush stays clear

what of the basic meaning of the Crush—what is its role
in life

without the Crush, all water would remain forever in the sea

Strongbox Letter #77

without you

in this world to receive

the O's and I's

the hard carbon

of my desire

How to Love a Married Woman

Radio silence means either passion or dispassion.

The ointment in the cabinet evades your reach.

She will never tassel her window with your blue flag.

Pull your own lamp closer, glean her words late into the night.

Learn how grass leaves sheath the organ they subtend: you are grass
    and outermost sheath: your organs are failing: you remember
    subtending her: how easily divisible her soul.

You are way beyond the point of favors.

Plan to die without her by your side.

Diffusely branched is still branched. Is branched. Branched.

I Want to Tell Rachel Carson about Neutrinos

Except how to tell a woman who died of breast cancer
about particles (Ve Vμ Vτ) so small they pass undetected
through every square inch of matter every second?

"Prove it," she might say, as she dips a toe into the lake
from the edge of the dock. "Prove it," she'd insist.
So I'd put my fishing pole down and admit the idea
resembles more a Buddhist's take on emotion than any
dog-eared hypothesis.

Still, despite my skill with conflation,
I'd lack sufficient language to satisfy her.
Even the word "neutrino" sounds like too much of a muchness,
but "oh," I'd say, "oh, how they stream, Rachel, such silent,
spiraling queerness."

It might help her to know that some things move through us
and don't alter a single cell, don't metastasize and shave off years,
don't settle in the breast and forge a second sun.

"Not antimatter," I'd say (though there are antineutrinos),
"but particles, grouped by 'flavors.'" How they whirr, Rachel,
through heartwood and rot alike,
through the water with her ashes,
through my laptop as I put it down to join her
and the loons in the lake.

The Sea around Us

a cento, from Rachel Carson's book of the same title

V.

The sea—local matter

that begins wholly

outside the earth.

XI.

Inaccessible empire   cheerless before   the ancient
Polynesians colonized the Pacific   sailing above a thousand
Mississippis   that tongue and curl   around caves drowned

I.

It is a curious fact, tide.

Pattern not of water

but energy.

A wave's one essential quality—
it moves.

Remember, Body

two women in the night water
write on each other
phosphorescent words.

First, single syllables:
once, you, breath,

then one of them tries *lavender*
and runs out of collarbone.

That time of year, dawn arrives earlier
every day. It arrives and arrives and arrives.

One of those women shivers
like a fortune teller
married to a doctor
on the eve of an epidemic.

The tide always rolls back out,
and with its wash,
any creature without
something to hold onto.

NOTES

The title "Remember, Body" is from the title of a book by C. P. Cavafy of the same name.

The fragments in "Epistles in Which Rachel Carson Uses Romantic Language" are excerpted from *Always, Rachel: The Letters of Rachel Carson and Dorothy Freeman, 1952–1964,* edited by Martha E. Freeman.

In the poem "Strongbox Letter #46," the phrase "the money's in mammals" is from *On a Farther Shore: The Life and Legacy of Rachel Carson, Author of Silent Spring* by William Souder.

The title of the poem "Why Rachel Carson Was Not a Painter" was inspired by the Frank O'Hara poem "Why I Am Not a Painter."

The phrase "the plural of anecdote is data" is attributed to political scientist Raymond Wolfinger.

The phrase "what thoughts I have of you tonight, Rachel Carson," in "The Plural of Anecdote Is Data," is a nod to Allen Ginsberg's line "what thoughts I have of you tonight, Walt Whitman."

The image "trace your hand on a piece of paper" in the poem "How to Love a Famous Woman" is inspired by one of the many anecdotes told to me by the kind docent at the Rachel Carson Homestead.

In the poem "Cento in Which the Word 'Cloud' Is Replaced by the Word 'Crush,'" I use Rachel Carson's language for a 1957 television show "Something about the Sky." The script is reprinted in *Lost Woods: The Discovered Writing of Rachel Carson* by Roger Allen Christie, and courtesy of Frances Collin, trustee.

ACKNOWLEDGMENTS

Thank you to the editors of the following journals in which these poems first appeared, some under different titles:

Grist: "How to Love a Famous Woman" (as "How to Love the Natural Sciences")

Poet Lore: "I Want to Tell Rachel Carson About Centralia, Pennsylvania, & 24-Hour Gas Stations"

The Rumpus: "I Want to Tell Rachel Carson About Rape Culture," "The Poet Discovers That Nothing Bad Ever Happened at Rachel Carson's Childhood Home," and "Pygmalion" (as "The Poet Admits to Playing Pygmalion with the Archive")

Shenandoah: "Epistles in Which Rachel Carson Uses Romantic Language That Will Worry Biographers Claiming Her Relationship with Dorothy Freeman Was Strictly Platonic: A Cento" and "Remember, Body"

The Shore: "Fundamental" (as "Juvenilia"), "Leaving Pennsylvania for the Sea (as "The Marine Biologist Leaves Springdale, Pennsylvania, For the Sea"), and "Some Mothers Are as Lighthouse to Ship"

The Southern Review: "Rachel Carson Considers the Family Homestead" and "Deathbed" (as "Rachel Carson at the Deathbed of Mary Scott Skinker")

Split Rock Review: "Why Rachel Carson Was Not a Painter" (as "Why the Marine Biologist Was Not a Painter")

"I Want to Tell Rachel Carson About Centralia, Pennsylvania, & 24-Hour Gas Stations" was nominated by *Poet Lore* for *Best New Poets 2022* and selected by Editor Paula Bohince and Jeb Livingood, Series Editor.

This book exists because of the many midwives, cheerleaders, and mentors that I've been lucky to encounter in my life, more than I can name. But it's an honor to try.

Thank you to Bob Hicok for selecting this book, and to William Waltz and Conduit Books & Ephemera for bringing it into the world.

I'm also grateful for the financial and/or intellectual support provided by the University of Colorado Denver, the Reisher Foundation, Purdue University, the Rachel Carson Homestead, the Edmund S. Muskie Archives and Special Collections Library at Bates College, Bucknell University, the fellows and faculty at the Stadler Center for Poetry & Literary Arts, Texas Tech University, and the Helen Jones Foundation.

I'm grateful for the wild places that provided sanity and space to write so many of these poems, including and especially Prophetstown, Muleshoe, Shakamak, and Barr Lake; and to Diane Chick and Jeff DeHaven, whose gift of place made some of these poems possible.

Thank you to the teachers and mentors that have instructed, inspired, and encouraged me: Joanna Luloff, Wayne Miller, Nicky Beer, Brian Barker, Teague Bolan, Marianne Boruch, Donald Platt, Brian Leung, Curtis Bauer, Cordelia Barrera, and Chris Taylor.

Thank you to the following people whose brilliant, compassionate insights into what it means to be human have provided me with endless inspiration: Kristin and Cory Wright-Bettner, Shauna Musser, Kelsey Carmody-Wart, Jenn Thompson, Javan DeHaven, Angela Monteith, Misha Bogart, Dakota Stranik, Noah Baldino, Daschielle Louis, Katie McMorris, Lucas Hunter, Vitasta Singh, Josh Luckenbach, Caleb Braun, Emma Aylor, Sara Ryan, Eytan Pol, Julie Grandjean, and Bria Winfree. A huge thank you to the rest of the Purdue crew; my first writing cohort at CU Denver; and my forestry crew—Jamie, Scott, and Margarita (y'all were shaping me and this book before I knew it). Lastly, but not in the least, I'm grateful to the many students that have brought their earnest and compassionate insights to the classroom.

Thank you, Chet'la Sebree, for the insightful blurb, and for modeling rigor, grace, and curiosity as a mentor.

Thank you, Kaveh Akbar, transcendent Iranian-American poet, ultimate cheerleader, and force of nature, for your relentless support of me and my writing. Your brilliance and generosity light these pages.

Endless love for my ride-or-die family: Dad, Jes, and Sara. And to my mom, who would have been proud to see my first book in the world.

My everything to Patrick. You are that boy on the baseball field in Brighton whose belief and love makes me feel that anything is possible.

This book is dedicated to Rachel Carson, biologist, writer, low-key trail blazer: thank you for being both lodestar and enigma.

ABOUT THE AUTHOR

Based in Colorado, Jennifer Loyd is a poet, translator, and a former editor for *Copper Nickel, West Branch,* and *Sycamore Review.* For her poetry exploring the archives of Rachel Carson, she has received a Stadler Fellowship, as well as travel grants for research from Purdue University, where she earned an MFA. Her poems and prose, which explore the intersection between private voice and public narratives, appear in *Best New Poets 2022, The Southern Review, The Rumpus, Shenandoah, Prairie Schooner, Poet Lore,* and elsewhere.

OTHER TITLES FROM CONDUIT BOOKS & EPHEMERA

Bright Life, Animal Heart by Laura Minor

Beneath All Water by Zackary Medlin

Extremely Expensive Mystical Experiences for Astronauts by Dara Barrois/Dixon

Autoblivion by Trey Moody

The Art of Bagging by Joshua Gottlieb-Miller

Thunderbird Inn by Collin Callahan

The Birthday of the Dead by Rachel Abramowitz

The World to Come by David Keplinger

Present Tense Complex by Suphil Lee Park

Sacrificial Metal by Esther Lee

The Miraculous, Sometimes by Meg Shevenock

The Last Note Becomes Its Listener by Jeffrey Morgan

Animul/Flame by Michelle Lewis